A Note to Parents

DK READERS is a compelling program for beginning readers, designed in conjunction with leading literacy experts, including Dr. Linda Gambrell, Distinguished Professor of Education at Clemson University. Dr. Gambrell has served as President of the National Reading Conference, the College Reading Association, and the International Reading Association.

Beautiful illustrations and superb full-color photographs combine with engaging, easy-to-read stories to offer a fresh approach to each subject in the series. Each DK READER is guaranteed to capture a child's interest while developing his or her reading skills, general knowledge, and love of reading.

The five levels of DK READERS are aimed at different reading abilities, enabling you to choose the books that are exactly right for your child:

Pre-level 1: Learning to read
Level 1: Beginning to read
Level 2: Beginning to read alone
Level 3: Reading alone
Level 4: Proficient readers

The "normal" age at which a child begins to read can be anywhere from three to eight years old. Adult participation through the lower levels is very helpful for providing encouragement, discussing storylines, and sounding out unfamiliar words.

No matter which level you select, you can be sure that you are helping your child learn to read, then read to learn!

LONDON, NEW YORK, MUNICH,
MELBOURNE, AND DELHI

Series Editor Deborah Lock
U.S. Editor John Searcy
Art Editor Mary Sandberg
Managing Art Editor Rachael Foster
Production Editor Sean Daly
Production Claire Pearson
Picture Researcher Harriet Mills
Jacket Designer Natalie Godwin

Reading Consultant
Linda Gambrell, Ph.D.

First American Edition, 2009
09 10 11 12 13 10 9 8 7 6 5 4 3 2
Published in the United States by DK Publishing
375 Hudson Street, New York, New York 10014

DK books are available at special discounts when purchased
in bulk for sales promotions, premiums,
fund-raising, or educational use.
For details, contact: DK Publishing Special Markets
375 Hudson Street, New York, New York 10014
SpecialSales@dk.com

A catalog record for this book is available
from the Library of Congress
ISBN: 978-0-7566-4522-9 (Paperback)
ISBN: 978-0-7566-4523-6 (Hardcover)

Color reproduction by Colourscan, Singapore
Printed and bound in China by L. Rex Printing Co. Ltd.

The publisher would like to thank the following for their kind
permission to reproduce their photographs:
(Key: a-above; b-below/bottom; c-center; l-left; r-right; t-top)
Alamy Images: John Angerson 28b; Paul Collis 8-9 (main image);
Danita Delimont 9tr, 12-13, 25tr, 32tl; Franck Fotos 31cr; JTB Photo
Communications, Inc/Haga Library 16-17; Tom Mackie 26-27; Jeff
Morgan alternative technology 23tr; Photofusion Picture Library 3c;
The Photolibrary Wales 10-11, 11tr, 32cla; Robert Harding Picture
Library Ltd 13tr; Henry Westheim Photography 14, 15tr. **Corbis:** Jean
Pierre Amet/Sygma 30; Getty Images: Jeremy Horner/Riser 17t;
Photonica/Franco Zecchin 7bl, 32clb; Stuart Westmorland/Stone 24-25.
Imagestate: Goran Burenhult 18cl, 32cl. **naturepl.com:** Eric Baccega 6,
7, 35br; Constantinos Petrinos 18-19 (main image), 19tr. **Robert Estall
Photo Library:** Carol Beckwith & Angela Fisher 22 (main image).
Shutterstock: Clouston 21br, 32bl; Dana E. Fry 5; Andy Z. 4.
Still Pictures: K. Hennig 27

Jacket images: *Front: Photolibrary:* Franck Guiziou.
Back: **Shutterstock:** Clouston tr. **naturepl.com:** Eric Baccega tl.
All other images © Dorling Kindersley
For further information see: www.dkimages.com

Discover more at
www.dk.com

Contents

BEGINNING 1 TO READ

Homes
Around the World

Written by Max Moore

DK Publishing

Most of us live in houses or apartment buildings.

They are usually made of bricks
or concrete.

But not all homes in the world
are like this.
Some people live in unusual
homes.

Would you like to live high
above the ground?
Some people who live in forests
and jungles build treehouses.

They use bamboo, vines, and
wood from the forest to make
their homes.

treehouse

Imagine you could go outside,
dig up some clay, and
use it to build a house.
People in very hot places
can do this.

The sun dries
the clay into strong
adobe bricks.

adobe

These cone-shaped mud-brick homes are called beehive houses. Their tall, cone-shaped roofs help keep them cool inside.

All the hot air
rises to the top
of the house.

beehive house

What would it be like to live
on a lake?
Some people build their homes
on floating islands made of reeds.

They add a layer of fresh reeds every few months.

reeds

Some fishermen build
wooden houses on stilts
over the water.
People walk along boardwalks
to get to stores, work, and school.

boardwalk

Houses on stilts are also
sometimes built on land.
People walk up a ramp
to get into their homes.
Cows, pigs, horses,
and chickens are kept
under the houses.

stilts

ramp

Would you like a house shaped like a boat?
These wooden houses are called tongkonans.
These are the homes of the Toraja people.

tongkonan

Some houses have many carvings of plants and animals inside.

Have you ever moved to
a new house?
Some people move several times
every year.

They can fold up their houses
and set them up again
somewhere else.
These houses are covered with
  animal skins.

yurt

Straw tents can be moved, too.
Straw is a light material but
is also strong, warm, and doesn't
let water in.

Straw can also be used to make the walls of homes that don't move.

Imagine living in a very cold place.
People used to build houses
from blocks of snow
to live in during the winter.

These igloos kept out the wind and were warm inside.

In hot places, some people live
in houses carved into rocks.
Cave homes are warm
in the winter
and cool in
the summer.

Some people build houses
in ways that help the planet.

This house is heated only by
the sun.

This house is made from
old shipping containers.

These houses use less energy
and material than most homes.

Some people build silly houses
just for fun.
These homes are made
to look like a mound of bubbles
and an alien spaceship.

In the future, people may build their homes in other unusual ways.

Glossary

Adobe
a material made from dried earth and straw

Beehive house
a cone-shaped mud-brick house

Tongkonan
a wooden house shaped like a boat

Treehouse
a house built high up in the trees

Yurt
a round home that can be moved around

THE BIG
WHITE GHOST

Adapted by Gail Herman

From the television script "Boo!" by Lois Becker and Mark Stratton

Illustrated by Ken Edwards

Based on the Scholastic book series
"Clifford The Big Red Dog"
by Norman Bridwell

No part of this publication may be reproduced in whole or in part, or stored in a retrieval system, or transmitted in any form or by any means, electronic, mechanical, photocopying, recording, or otherwise, without written permission of the publisher. For information regarding permission, write to Scholastic Inc., Attention: Permissions Department, 557 Broadway, New York, NY 10012.

ISBN 0-439-41682-5

18 17 16 15   14 15 16 17

Printed in the U.S.A.   40
First printing, September 2003

SCHOLASTIC INC.

New York   Toronto   London   Auckland   Sydney
Mexico City   New Delhi   Hong Kong   Buenos Aires

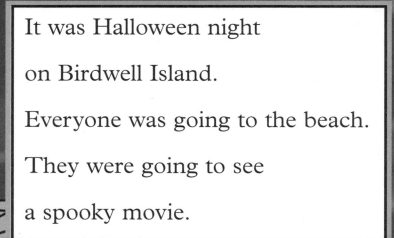

It was Halloween night

on Birdwell Island.

Everyone was going to the beach.

They were going to see

a spooky movie.